HOW TO BECOME ONE WITH YOUR MATE

Lawrence J. Crabb

PYRANEE
BOOKS

Zondervan Publishing House
Grand Rapids, Michigan

How to Become One with Your Mate

This book is excerpted from *The Marriage Builder*, copyright © 1982 by Lawrence J. Crabb.

This is a Pyranee Book
Published by the Zondervan Publishing House,
1415 Lake Drive, S.E., Grand Rapids, Michigan 49506

Library of Congress Cataloging in Publication Data

Crabb, Lawrence J.
    How to become one with your mate.

    Excerpted from Crabb's The marriage builder.
    "A Pyranee book"—T.p. verso.
    Includes bibliographical references.
    1. Marriage—Religious aspects—Christianity. I. Crabb,
Lawrence J. Marriage builder. II. Title.
BV835.C69 1986   248.8'4   86-18999
ISBN 0-310-22592-2

Printed in the United States of America

90 / 10 9 8 7

Contents

1

Oneness: What It Is and Why It Is Important

Several months ago I was working on a rough draft of this book during a flight to New York City. A flight attendant noticed the words "The Goal of Marriage" written at the top of a yellow pad of paper resting on the tray table in front of me. She asked what I was writing. When I told her I was starting a book on marriage, she said, "Well, I'm glad, because I really believe in marriage. After six years of living with a man, I decided that I wanted to be married. Since the fellow I was living with liked our no-strings-attached arrangement, I found somebody else who was willing to tie the knot, and we got married two months ago. So far it's great!"

I asked her why she preferred a marriage commitment to merely living together. She thought for a few seconds, then said, "I think it's the commitment part I wanted. I married a man who seems to be really committed to loving me and working on a relationship. I never felt secure enough to really open up and try to get close with a man who wouldn't make any promises."

This incident prompts two questions: (1) What was this woman's purpose in exchanging her live-in boyfriend for a husband? (2) How was she hoping to reach her objective?

Consider a second example.

A husband in his early thirties complained to me that his wife was a disappointment to him. She was pretty and personable, a good cook, and a devoted mother to their two

1

small children. But these qualities were offset by her constant criticizing, her impatient corrections and rebukes, and her negative attitude. Nothing he did seemed to satisfy her and, he added with a touch of noble frustration, he was the sort of husband many women would be delighted to have.

This man's wife had been staring dejectedly at the floor the whole time he was speaking. When he stopped talking, she spoke without raising her head. "What he says is true. I'm an awful nag, and I do complain a lot. I just feel so unloved by Jimmy."

When she raised her head, there was anger in her eyes.

"Sometimes he explodes at me, calling me awful names. He'll never pray with me. Sure, he smiles at me a lot, and he thinks that makes him a great husband, but I know he doesn't really accept me. His smiles always turn into pushy demands for sex; and when I won't give in to him, he throws a fit."

Reflect on this couple and ask the same two questions: (1) What was each partner longing for from the other? (2) What were their strategies for gaining their desires?

Think about one more illustration.

A middle-aged couple—Christians, attractive, talented, financially comfortable, faithful, active church members—admitted that their marriage was in trouble.

"I feel like such a hypocrite," the wife stated. "If you asked the people in our church to list the ten most happily married couples they know, our names would probably appear on every list. We're sociable, we entertain church people frequently in our beautiful home, we sing in the choir together. We really play the role—but our relationship is miserable.

"We get along—but from a distance. I can never tell him how I really feel about anything. He always gets mad and jumps at me, or he clams up for a couple days. I don't think we've ever had a really close relationship."

Her husband responded, "I don't think it's all that bad.

We've got a lot going for us: the kids are doing fine, my wife teaches Sunday school, the Lord is blessing my business. That's better than a lot of—

I interrupted. "How much do you really share yourself—your feelings, hopes, and dreams—with your wife?"

"Well," he answered, "whenever I try she usually doesn't seem all that interested, so I just don't bother."

"I'd listen if you'd really share with me!" his wife blurted. "But your idea of sharing is to lecture me on how things should be. Whenever I try to tell you how I feel, you always say something like "I don't know why you feel like that.' I think our communication is awful."

Once more, consider the same two questions: (1) What do these emotionally divorced partners want from their marriage but have so far been unable to develop? (2) How are they trying to achieve what they both so deeply desire?

The Need For Intimacy

Let's deal with the first question: *What was each of these people seeking?*

It is apparent that the flight attendant married in the hope that a relationship of mutual commitment would provide the intimacy she lacked with her live-in boyfriend.

The frustrated husband wanted to feel a sense of oneness with his wife but believed her critical and rejecting spirit was getting in the way. He felt angry with her, much as I would feel toward someone who, after I had gone without food for several days, blocked my path to a table spread with good things to eat. His wife felt unable to give herself warmly to a man who seemed to use rather than accept her. She desperately wanted to be close to her husband, but felt a sense of dread at the prospect of moving toward a man who perhaps didn't really love her.

The couple whose marriage was a well-decorated but empty package felt completely blocked from touching one another emotionally. The absence of real intimacy left a void for them—which she freely and bitterly acknowledged, but which he ignored by focusing on the external trappings of family success.

The newlywed stewardess, the explosive husband and his critical wife, and the couple who could not communicate were all pursuing the same elusive goal: *A deep experience of personal intimacy through relationship with a person of the opposite sex.*

People everywhere long for intimate relationships. We all need to be close to someone. Make no apology for your strong desire to be intimate with someone; it is neither sinful nor selfish. Don't ignore the need by preoccupying yourself with peripheral satisfactions such as social achievement or acquiring knowledge. Neglecting your longing for relationship by claiming to be above it is as foolish as pretending you can live without food. Our need for relationship is real, and it is there by God's design.

God created us in His image, personal beings unlike all other creatures, and like Him in our unique capacity for relationship. As dependent personal beings, we cannot function fully as we are designed without close relationships. I understand the Scriptures to teach that relationship offers two elements which are absolutely essential if we are to live as God intended: (1) The *security* of being truly loved and accepted, and (2) The *significance* of making a substantial, lasting, positive impact on another person.

The Problem of Feelings

To avoid misunderstanding, let me state that we do not need to *feel* secure or significant in order to function as we should. I may not *feel* worthy or accepted, but I am still responsible to *believe* what God has said. His Word assures me that in Christ I am both secure in His love and significant in His plan. A wife who *feels* desperately insecure is quite capable of giving herself to her husband if she *believes* she is secure in Christ. A husband who *feels* threatened by his

4

wife's rejection is responsible for lovingly accepting her because he can *believe* that he is a worthwhile Christian regardless of his wife's response.

Christ has made me secure and significant. Whether I feel it or not, it is true. I am instructed by God to believe that my needs are already met, and therefore I am to live selflessly, concerned only with the needs of others. The more I choose to live according to the truth of what Christ has done for me, the more I will come to sense the reality of my security and significance in Him.

Sin has made an utter wreck of things. God's original design was that man and woman should live in fellowship with Him and in a selfless relationship of mutual giving to each other. In such a relationship my love would so thrill my wife that I would feel deeply *significant* as I realized the joy that my love creates in her; I would exult in the *security* that her love provides me. She too would find her *significance* in touching my deepest needs and would enjoy the *security* of my love for her.

But something has gone wrong in our marriage. I no longer believe that my needs are already met. I seem to think that I need my spouse to give me security and significance *before* I can respond as I should. I now *wait* for her to fill me first, *then* I give of myself to her. If she fails to come through in a way that satisfies me, I back away or perhaps attack her. To the degree that I trust her to accept me fully, I will be open and loving with her. But now my love for her depends on her love for me. And she approaches our relationship in exactly the same way. *If* I love her in a way that brings her security, *then* she gives herself in loving subjection to me. Otherwise she establishes enough distance to numb the pain of rejection.

A terrible situation results. Because I have asked my spouse to meet my needs, she now has the power to withhold what I need—and thereby to destroy me. *Fear* has entered our relationship. We have become afraid of each other. We play cat-and-mouse, wait-and-see games. Neither of us can find what we desperately need in our relationship because of fear.

Yet God intends that I become one with my wife in a relationship that deeply touches her need for security. And she is to become one with me in a way that satisfies my longing for significance and worth. God planned for our marriage to develop into an intimate relationship in which we experience the truth that our deepest personal needs for significance and security are genuinely met in Christ. When God presented Eve to her husband, the Bible tells us, they became one flesh, that is, they fully experienced a relationship of *Oneness*. Developing this kind of relationship is the goal of marriage.

The goal of oneness can be almost frightening when we realize that God does not intend that my wife and I find our personal needs met in our marriage. He also wants our relationship to validate the claims of Christianity to a watching world as an example of the power of Christ's redeeming love to overcome the divisive effects of sin. In John 17:21, Jesus poured out His heart to the Father: "I pray . . . that all of them may be one, Father, just as you are in me and I am in you. May they also be in us so that the world may believe that you have sent me." Our relationships with all fellow believers were in mind in Christ's prayer for oneness; but marriage, with its unique opportunity for intimacy, offers a convincing demonstration of the power of Christ's love to enable people to experience true relationship.

The first of our two questions can now be answered more completely. What were the stewardess and the two unhappy couples seeking? A relationship in which their deepest needs for security and significance could be substantially met.

Now, the second question: How were they trying to develop such a relationship?

Whatever strategies the two couples had followed were

6

woefully ineffective. Neither am I confident that the flight attendant had a more successful game plan for achieving the oneness she desired.

What is an effective strategy for building a good relationship? Should you start by telling your partner everything you feel? Do you make a list of "ways to be nice this week" and do your best to follow it? Will getting up earlier to spend more time with God in devotions be helpful? Perhaps counseling or attending another seminar will do the trick. Or is the solution simply to repent of your selfishness and promise God to really do your part?

There are no simple answers. But there are answers—difficult to accept because they cut across the grain of our fallen human nature, and authoritative because they come from God's Word. The rest of this book attempts to provide these answers.

2

Spirit Oneness: Who Meets My Needs?

A man in his middle forties complained to me that his wife was cold, angry, and argumentative. I interrupted his recitation of her faults to say, "It sounds as if you think that because your wife is failing you so badly, you are therefore justified in your bitter attitude toward her. The Bible, however, instructs you to love your wife though she may be thoroughly disagreeable, to love her the way Christ loves His people."

He was incredulous.

"Wait a minute! Maybe I am supposed to love her— I'm sure I should. But I need a little love and respect too. She's giving me nothing but criticism and a cold shoulder, and you tell me to love her. Who's going to meet *my* needs?"

His question must not be lightly dismissed with exhortations to stop such self-centered fussing and to trust the Lord with whatever emotional bruises result from his wife's neglect. Truth reduced to the level of cliché ("Trust the Lord," "Pray about it," etc.) rarely promotes conviction or healing. This man has substantive needs that cry for satisfaction and will not quiet down under glib scolding and reminding that "Jesus is all you need."

This man was distraught and irritated as a result of his wife's failure to love him. The marriage relationship was not meeting his emotional needs. The solution to his problem seemed obvious to him: to change his wife so that she would meet his needs.

Picture the dilemma of the marriage counselor. Suppose he were to tell this man's wife that she should become more loving to her husband. Can you predict her response? "But I have needs too, and I don't feel very loved in this relationship either. Who's going to meet *my* needs for love and affection?"

To understand God's design for marriage, we must begin with the fact that both husbands and wives have legitimate personal needs which press for satisfaction.

These *personal* needs are as real as our *physical* needs. It is impossible to function effectively if these needs are not met. In this chapter I show that no marriage can ever follow the biblical pattern unless both partners have experienced satisfaction at the deepest level of their personal needs. These needs can only be met in the context of a relationship with someone else; no person can satisfy his own needs.

The Dilemma of Needs

This state of affairs creates a dilemma. Both my wife and I have real personal needs for love and respect that must be met if we are to treat each other as we should. It follows that I cannot fully love her until I sense that I am a loved, worthwhile person. It also follows that she cannot truly love me until she knows that she is a deeply secure woman. What are we to do?

Can I rightly rebuke my wife and exhort her to do better? But I really cannot expect her to treat me properly until she feels loved. Yet I am unable to provide her with the love *she* needs until someone meets *my* needs. This situation between husband and wife is rather like two bankrupt businessmen depending on each other for the capital to begin a new partnership.

Perhaps we are both supposed to rely exclusively on the Lord to respond adequately to our longings. This answer seems sound, but it has its own set of problems. The spiritual maturity required to experience Christ's love as continually

9

sustaining amid real emotional pain is a distant goal for many Christians. The Lord sometimes seems far off and removed from the reality of our pressing, human needs. A thirty-five-year-old woman whose husband has coldly neglected her for years has, understandably, a difficult time turning down a man who offers her a warm, close relationship that includes sexual relations. To console her with words about God's unfailing love seems rather like encouraging a starving woman by showing her magazine pictures of a well-spread dinner table; to exhort her to remain obedient to God's Word may somehow seem to deny or understate her legitimate hunger.

But suppose we commit ourselves to trusting fully in the sufficiency of Christ to meet our needs. What role, then, should our spouses assume? Is my wife to be only a concerned bystander watching from a distance as I struggle to deepen my walk with the Lord? Will her efforts to become close to God be so personal and private that I will be excluded from the realm of her innermost emotional nature? Exactly how are we to become deeply one?

Before we deal with these questions, we need to consider in greater detail the nature of personal needs.

Personal Needs

People are more than physical bodies. The Bible clearly teaches that our skin and bones and hair and organs constitute a home in which our personal selves temporarily live. When our hearts stop beating and our bodies decompose, that identifiable entity I know as "Me" continues in a conscious and personal existence. Who is this "Me"?

Genesis 1:27 states that mankind was created in God's image. In some sense, people are like God. But God is a non-corporeal being, that is, He does not have a physical body (except, of course, through the incarnation of the Second Person of the Godhead). His essential being is not matter. Therefore our similarity to God cannot be found in our flesh and bones. My *physical* being is not like God.

10

But I am a *personal* being, and that is like God. God is a loving, purposeful *Person* who thinks, chooses, and feels. I too am a *person* capable of love and purpose who thinks, chooses, and feels. The Bible uses various words to describe the personal character of man, such as *soul, mind, heart* and *will.* The biblical term *spirit,* however, seems to refer to the deepest part of man's essential nature as a person. When I think about the deepest part of me—the part that has the capacity for fellowship with God—I am reflecting on my spirit. Let us consider the characteristics of this person or spirit who resides in the body.

I recently asked a group of people to close their eyes and meditate on these questions: What do I really want? What are my deepest longings? What do I most desire that would bring me the greatest joy? As they meditated, I asked them to choose one word that best expressed their longings. Among the words they offered were *acceptance, meaning, love, purpose, value,* and *worth.*

Most of us, when we look within, can put our fingers on a strong desire to love and be loved, to accept and be accepted. When we sense that someone genuinely cares about us, or when we ourselves sense a deep compassion for someone else, something profound is stirred within us. I suggest that our longing for love represents one set of needs that partly defines what it means to be a person or spirit.

If you continue to reflect on your inner desires, you may notice something else. Do you experience an intangible sense of wholeness, a feeling of vitality and fullness, when you do something important to you? Washing dishes or mowing the lawn may bore us, but wrestling with decisions of major consequence or responding to a medical emergency extends into deeper parts of our personality. We sense an urgent meaningfulness to what we are doing—nerve-shattering perhaps, but meaningful. Thus, to be a person involves a second set of needs—needs for meaning and value.

The image of God is reflected in these two needs. God

11

is a personal being who in His essential nature is *love* and who, as a God of design and purpose, is the author of *meaning*. We too are personal beings, but unlike our infinite, self-sufficient, and perfect God, we are limited, dependent, and fallen. God *is* love; we *need* love. Whatever God does *is* significant; we *need to do* something significant.

We can state these needs succinctly:

Security: A convinced awareness of being unconditionally and totally loved without needing to change in order to win love, loved by a love that is freely given, that cannot be earned and therefore cannot be lost.

Significance: A realization that I am engaged in a responsibility or job that is truly important, whose results will not evaporate with time but will last through eternity, that fundamentally involves having a meaningful impact on another person, a job for which I am completely adequate.

Thus, being a person (or spirit) centrally involves an identity that requires security and significance to function effectively. When both these needs are met, we experience ourselves as *worthwhile* people.

My wife too is a spirit being, that is, she also needs to find security and significance. If we as a married couple are to become one at the level of our spirits—achieve what I call Spirit Oneness—then we must find some way to meet at the level of our deepest needs.

But how? And here we are back to the question posed at the beginning of this chapter: How can husband and wife become deeply one at the level of their personal needs? It would appear that as we seek to meet our personal needs in marriage, essentially four courses of action are open to us. We may—

1. Ignore our needs;
2. Find satisfaction in achievement;
3. Attempt to meet our needs in each other;
4. Depend on the Lord to meet our needs.

12

Option 1: Ignore our needs.

The first option can be quickly rejected. If, as I believe the Scriptures teach, these personal needs are as real as our physical needs for food, water, and shelter, then to ignore them is to invite catastrophe. When physical needs remain unmet, we move toward *physical death*. When personal needs for security and significance are neglected and go unsatisfied, we move toward *personal death*. The symptoms of approaching personal death include feelings of worthlessness, despair, morbid fears, loss of motivation and energy, a turning to drugs or sex or alcohol to numb the pain of dying, and a sense of emptiness and boredom. We have been created with real personal needs and, to be faithful stewards of our lives, we must not ignore them.

Option 2: Find satisfaction in achievement.

Operating through a fallen world, Satan has taught us to believe a lie. Our culture encourages us to measure a person's value by his or her achievement. The world has squeezed many Christians into the mold of believing that our need for a sense of worth can be met without entering into a deep relationship with the living God.

Too many couples have unwittingly bought Satan's lie. The "beautiful people" who have been blessed with money, good looks, and talent may experience a counterfeit sense of worth that provides some satisfaction of their needs. Because the pain of their unmet needs is dulled, they may never enter into the difficult struggle of finding real security and significance. Their lives may appear happy, vital, and trouble-free—no morbid wrestling matches with deep inner conflict. Whenever discomfort reaches the threshold of awareness, these people anesthetize it with more activities, purchases, trips, or whatever else they enjoy.

I wonder how many Christian couples with comfortable means and interesting lives never come together at the deepest level of their personalities, but bury their inward longings for love and purpose under a mountain of success instead.

13

How sad! How empty! Better to struggle with substance than to comfortably accept a shadow.

Following Option 2—attempting to find satisfaction in achievement rather than in the struggles of relationship—will reliably result in a shallow relationship that may feel very pleasant but will fail to unite husband and wife at their deepest level.

Option 3: Attempt to meet our needs in each other.

If ignoring our needs is dangerous and if finding counterfeit satisfaction in achievement results in shallow relationships, then what should we do with our needs? A large majority of people turn to their marriage partners for the answer.

Consider what may really be happening when a couple get married: Two people, each with personal needs pressing for fulfillment, pledge themselves to become one. As they recite their vows to love and respect each other, strong but hidden motivations stir inside them. If a tape recorder could somehow tune into the couple's unconscious intentions, I wonder if perhaps we would hear words like these:

> *Bridegroom:* I need to feel important and I expect you to meet that need by submitting to my every decision, whether good or bad; by respecting me no matter how I behave; and by supporting me in whatever I choose to do. I want you to treat me as the most important man in the world. My goal in marrying you is to find my significance through you. An arrangement in which you are commanded by God to submit to me sounds very attractive.
>
> *Bride:* I have never felt as deeply loved as my nature requires. I am expecting you to meet that need through gentle affection even when I'm growling, thoughtful consideration whether I am always sensitive to you or not, and an accepting, romantic sensitivity to my emotional ups and downs. Don't let me down.

14

A marriage bound together by commitments to exploit the other for filling one's own needs (and I fear that most marriages are built on such a basis) can legitimately be described as a "tic on a dog" relationship. Just as a hungry tic clamps on to a nourishing host in anticipation of a meal, so each partner unites with the other in the expectation of finding what his or her personal nature demands. The rather frustrating dilemma, of course, is that in such a marriage there are two tics and no dog!

Inevitably, as the years pass, husband and wife will occasionally touch at deep levels. One woman told me how desperate she felt when the doctor emerged from the operating room to inform her that her four-year-old daughter had just died. In that moment she knew a terrible pain that penetrated to the core of her being. When she fell into her husband's arms, he coldly pushed her away and left the hospital. She was alone at a time when she needed to know that life still had purpose. When she needed to feel the love of someone close, her husband failed her. There is no greater torment than to expose your needs so fully and receive no help. And *every* husband and wife, no matter how godly, has many times failed to provide what the other has needed.

Reflect on your marriage for a moment. Is there a feeling of hurt that you are reluctant to share directly with your spouse or perhaps a subject (like sex or time together or annoying habits) that you carefully avoid? Why? Why do we sometimes have difficulty telling our spouses how we feel or what concerns us?

Every person alive has experienced sometime the profound hurt of finding rejection when he or she longed for acceptance. We come into marriage hoping for something different, but inevitably we soon encounter some form of criticism or rejection. The pain that results is so intense that it *demands* relief. So we retreat behind protective walls of emotional distance, angry with our partners for letting us down so badly, unwilling to meet again at the level of deep needs for fear of experiencing more pain.

A variety of behaviors can function as protective layers. Some of the more common ones, which we will discuss in chapter 3, are—

- Unwillingness to share deep feelings;
- Responding with anger when real feelings are hurt;
- Changing the subject when the conversation begins to be threatening;
- Turning off, clamming up, or other maneuvers designed to avoid rejection or criticism;
- Keeping oneself so busy with work, social engagements, entertainment, church activities, or endless chatter that no deep sharing is possible.

Again, the point of each of these layers is to protect oneself from vulnerability to hurt at the hands of a spouse.

I am persuaded that most couples today live behind thick protective walls of emotional distance that block any hope for developing substantial oneness at the level of our deepest personal needs. What is to be done? Shouldn't we learn to be more loving and sensitive to each other? Can't we break down the barriers that separate us by accepting each other as God for Christ's sake has accepted us? Of course we should. The Bible tells us to and therefore we can. But we can never do it perfectly.

The most accepting wife in the world cannot meet her husband's need for significance. Because she is a sinner, my wife will not always minister to me as she should; even if she were to do so, she does not have the power to make me adequate for an eternally important task—and that alone will satisfy me.

The most loving husband in the world can never meet his wife's need for security. The stain of self-centeredness has discolored every motivation within us. We are utterly incapable of providing our wives with the unconditional and

16

selfless acceptance they require. We simply are not enough for each other.

Let me briefly restate the problems with Option 3. If I look to my wife to meet my needs, then our relationship is corrupted by (1) *manipulative efforts* to acquire what I think I need; (2) *fear* that my manipulations may not be effective; (3) *anger and pain* when they do not succeed; and (4) a nagging (perhaps unconscious) sense of *guilt* because my approach to marriage is fundamentally selfish. We will inevitably retreat from each other behind protective layers that block the development of oneness.

I am therefore forced to conclude that if my wife and I are to become one at the level of our spirit (the deepest level of our being), then we must *not* depend on each other to meet our personal needs. What are we to do?

Option 4: Depend on the Lord to meet our needs.

Our personal needs for security and significance can be genuinely and fully met only in relationship with the Lord Jesus Christ. To put it another way, all that we need to function effectively as persons *(not necessarily to feel happy or fulfilled)* is at any given moment fully supplied in relationship with Christ and in whatever He chooses to provide.

1. We need to be secure. He loves us with a love we never deserved, a love that sees everything ugly within us yet accepts us, a love that we can do nothing to increase or decrease, a love that was forever proven at the Cross, where Christ through His shed blood fully paid for our sins to provide us with the gift of an eternally loving relationship with God. In that love, I am secure.

2. We need to be significant. The Holy Spirit has graciously and sovereignly equipped every believer to participate in God's great purpose of bringing all things together in Christ. The body of Christ builds itself up through the exercise of each member's gifts. We are enabled to express our value by ministering to others, encouraging our spouses,

17

training our children, enduring wrong without grumbling, and faithfully doing everything to the limits of our capacity for the glory of God. We can live in the confidence that God has set out a path of good works for us to follow (Eph. 2:10) and that our obedience will contribute to fulfilling the eternal plan of God. These truths, when realized and acted upon, provide unparalleled significance.

The Platform of Truth

Our fourth option, then, is to depend on the Lord to meet our personal needs. We really have no other rational choice. But there are problems. Our dulled eyes of faith strain to keep these spiritual realities in clear focus. We have a remarkable capacity for failing to lay hold of ideas that I suppose would seem so clear to undiluted faith.

Spiritual truth can be compared to a balance beam, a narrow platform from which we can easily fall off either side. The central truth that serves as the platform for Christian marriage—and for all Christian relationships—is that in Christ we are at every moment eternally loved and genuinely significant.

Too often Christians fall off this platform of truth into error. When key relationships (marriage, family, friendship) or life events (job, health, prestige) fail to make me *feel* secure or significant, it may be difficult to hold firmly onto the fact that I remain a worthwhile person. When a wife communicates disrespect for her husband or when a husband emotionally withdraws from his wife, it is not easy for the rejected partner to grasp with warm conviction the truth of acceptance and worth in Christ.

Thus, rejection and failure can easily nudge us off the platform of truth into Error 1: *Because someone has rejected me or because I have failed, I am less worthwhile as a person.*

It is also possible to slip from the platform of truth into error on the other side. The truth that "Christ is all I need" may sometimes degenerate into a defensive posture to avoid personal hurt by maintaining a safe emotional distance in relationships. I once heard a lonely but proud man say to a Christian colleague, "Because I have Jesus, I am worthwhile with or without you. Your criticism therefore doesn't get to me at all. Nor does your acceptance really matter to me. It would represent a lack of faith in the Lord to let you affect me emotionally." He fell headlong into Error 2: *Hiding behind the truth of our worth in Christ to avoid feeling pain in relationships.*

Regardless of our spiritual maturity, we will acutely feel the pain of loss and rejection. And rightly so. Although our central relationship is with the Lord, we should enter into relationships with others deep enough to cause profound hurt when they fail. To say that Christ is sufficient does *not* imply that He is to function as some sort of asbestos cover protecting us from the pain of interpersonal fire. Rather, His resources make it possible for us to continue responding biblically in spite of the great pain we may feel, because the hurt, though great, will never be enough to rob us of our security and significance. And all we need to live as Christians, no matter what our circumstances, is the security of His love and the significance of participation in His purpose. We must never claim that our relationships with others do not affect us deeply: they do. But Christ's resources are enough to keep us going.

In the rest of this chapter we will think through how a Christian couple can become spiritually one by remaining atop the platform of truth.

Consider first how we can avoid falling into Error 1.

What are Christian husbands and wives to do when they keenly feel the insensitivity or disrespect of their spouses? How can they handle the acute pain of felt insecurity or insignificance that seeks relief behind the protective layers of emotional distance? How can a spouse who *feels* hurt realistically hang onto the truth of personal worth in Christ and thus avoid falling into the first error?

A woman I was counseling came to realize that for years she had been turning to her children for emotional fulfillment. Her husband had shut her out of his life, leaving her hungry for affection and loving response. She found what she wanted in her children. This led to a stubborn reluctance to approach her husband with love and warmth, and the source of her reluctance was a profound fear that he would react coldly to her overtures.

I suggested that she was depending on her husband to meet her personal needs and that her relationship was essentially selfish and manipulative. She shook her head and answered, "I know God is supposed to meet my need for love, but what am I supposed to do with all this hurt and fear? I believe God loves me, but I can't get it to really work inside me."

I recommended that she follow three steps to help her find solid footing on the platform of the truth that because Christ loves her, she can be obedient to all that Scripture commands.

Step 1: Fully acknowledge all your feelings to God.

Christians are often trained to pretend that they feel joyful and happy when they are really miserable. Because we "shouldn't" feel unhappy, we pretend we don't. Yet Hebrews 4:15 teaches that our Great High Priest can sympathize with us when we experience weakness. How wrong it is, then, to hide our emotional weaknesses from Him and to deny ourselves the comfort of noncritical understanding.

I encouraged this woman to fully acknowledge her hurt and pain before God, to literally and openly express what she was feeling in God's presence. So often people respond to such advice by reciting in contrite tones a prayer like "Lord, please forgive me for feeling hurt." But this misses the point entirely. We are not to pretend that we feel *penitent* when we feel *hurt*. When our stomachs churn with grief or anger or pain, we must humbly acknowledge to the

One-who-sees-everything whatever we really feel. My client eventually prayed like this: "Lord, right now I am hurting more than I think I can endure. I feel like screaming, running away, hitting somebody! I don't want to feel this way, but I do. I feel worthless, empty, sad, and angry. Thank you for loving me exactly as I am."

Step 2: Reaffirm the truth of your security and significance in Christ.

One of the central truths of the Christian life is that our feelings need never determine how we believe or what we do. I exhorted this woman to remind herself that in Christ she is a fully loved and worthwhile woman despite her husband's rejection. To grasp this truth better, I asked her to picture her mind as a tape recorder. We observed that whenever her husband in some form rejected her, she immediately "played a tape" that said, "When my husband rejects me, my need for love cannot be met. I am dependent on my husband to make me feel loved."

The belief that Christ is not sufficient for our personal needs is a lie of Satan. I wrote a new "tape" on a card and asked her to play it (to repeat it to herself) the next time she perceived rejection from her husband. The new tape read: "My husband may reject me. If he does, I will hurt, perhaps a lot. But no matter how he treats me, I am at this moment totally and wonderfully loved by Christ. Because of His love, I am a secure woman."

Step 3: Commit yourself to ministering to your spouse's needs, knowing that however he may respond can never rob you of your worth as a person.

Because faith (playing the right tapes) is dead without works, the final step in helping my client to stand on the platform of truth was to encourage her to live out the implications of her new tape. Because she really is secure in

Christ, she can make herself vulnerable to her husband's rejection by giving herself fully to him. The fact that she has not done so is sin and must be confessed as such. Repentance must follow.

I asked her to picture a cliff. In her imagination she was to see herself standing on its edge looking down into the abyss. The abyss represents what she fears would destroy her: her husband's rejection. While she remains on the cliff, she is safe; she cannot experience the deep pain of her husband's rejection so long as she keeps her distance from him. Every time she backs away from him or lashes out at him or hides behind a protective layer, she is choosing to remain on the cliff of emotional safety.

We discussed the biblical model of marriage that requires her to give herself fully to her husband for the purpose of helping him feel valuable and important. To obey the Lord, she would need to jump off the cliff of safety and distance into her husband's rejecting arms. She looked at me with terror in her eyes: "If I give myself to him I'll get hurt again. And I just can't handle any more rejection!"

I then asked her to visualize a strong rope tied securely around her waist, a rope held by the Lord from His position directly over the abyss, with the rope representing God's love. As long as she remains on the cliff, the rope hangs limply, because it is not challenged by her weight. The cliff, not the rope, is supporting her.

It was apparent to my client that from her position on the cliff she could never *feel* the strength of the rope. To develop the conviction that "Christ's love really does make me secure," she would have to jump, to leave the cliff of safety by committing herself to meeting her husband's needs no matter what the cost. She cannot meaningfully claim that she is trusting the Lord for all her needs until she leaps from the cliff. Until she is dangling over the abyss of rejection, held only by the love of God—and not until then—will she deeply know that Christ can meet her need for security. He fear of rejection keeps her on the cliff. "Perfect love drives out fear" (1 John 4:18). But we will never know that love until we depend on it to preserve us from destruction.

My client studied the diagram. "I can really see what you mean. But it doesn't take away the fear. Even thinking about making that jump terrifies me."

Her comment triggered one more addition to the sketch. After a fearful person jumps from the cliff of safety, there is an *interval of time* before the rope of love extends fully to support the person's weight over the abyss. The situation is similar to skydiving. When a skydiver steps from the plane, he or she experiences a few moments of sheer, unsupported falling until the parachute opens. For the scared Christian who makes the "leap of faith," the moments before Christ's love is experienced as real personal security may last an hour, a day, a week, a year, or longer. During this interval between the jump and the felt reality of security in Christ, the Christian will likely sense a fear more profound than any known before. At this time, relying on the Word of God is absolutely indispensable. "Underneath are the everlasting arms" (Deut. 33:27). "My flesh and my heart may fail, but God is the strength of my heart" (Ps. 73:26).

The Problem of Emotional Withdrawal

Now consider how we can keep from slipping into Error 2. Falling from the platform into the second error ("Since Christ is all I need, I can withdraw from you emotionally") will destroy any hope of developing Spirit Oneness. Although it is true that our needs are fully met in Christ, it is also true that the Lord normally uses husbands and wives as His instruments to develop within each other a conscious awareness of personal worth. It is Christ alone who grants us security and significance, but it is often (by no means always) our spouses who help us to *feel* worthwhile.

God commands husbands and wives to submit to one another, that is, to put each other's *needs* first. I am to touch my spouse's deepest needs in such a way that I produce in her a conscious taste of what it is like to be deeply loved and respected.

Now, if we are to do our jobs well, we must explore how our behavior affects each other's awareness of our security and significance in Christ. In doing so, we will necessarily expose very private aspects of our personality. Nothing gives me a deeper sense of oneness with my wife than to share with her some of my struggles—the disappointments, hurts, fears, and unmet longings.

To know that she is aware of my most central struggles initially creates an incredible fear: I stand exposed and naked before her. Will she pass off my concerns lightly? Will she lose respect for me? Will she laugh or criticize? If she does reject me, I must depend on Christ's love as my basis for a sense of worth. But when she listens to me—really listens—and accepts me with my problems and frustrations, a closeness develops between us that can help me to regain the perspective to believe that I really am worthwhile in Christ. The kind of closeness that results from revealing to my wife central parts within me which I share with no one else is a central element in Spirit Oneness.

To remain atop the platform and to develop this kind of oneness, husbands and wives need to regard problems, not as a cause to withdraw, but rather as an opportunity to learn how to minister better to each other. Let me illustrate this truth with a personal example.

Some weeks ago, as my wife and I got into our car after a Bible study, she said in a voice mixed with anger and pain, "I really felt hurt tonight when you said . . . and now I'm so furious I can't even talk about it."

Exactly how does a person move from that beginning toward spiritual oneness? Consider a few of my options and select the one that you think would best develop closeness.

1. I could have ignored her, knowing that by morning she would settle down and speak politely and perhaps by

the next evening become warm again. Why discuss a subject that will just develop into an argument and make matters worse? After all, regardless of whether I failed her or not, I am still accepted by Christ.

2. I could defend myself: "Whatever I did, I didn't mean to hurt you." Or I could attack her: "Well, you hurt me, too" or "You are really sensitive. You ought to trust the Lord more" or "All right, tell me what you're mad about now."

3. I could attempt to cut short an anticipated painful conversation with a quick apology.

If you selected any of these options as good bets to improve your marriage, you need this book.

Regretfully, although I know better, I chose to respond with the second option of defense and attack. The conversation went something like this:

> *Me:* "What on earth did I do now? (Subtle attack on her oversensitivity)
> *Her:* "You put me down in front of the whole group when you said . . ."
> *Me:* "Honey, that was not a put-down! You completely misunderstood what I meant!" (Defend and attack)
> *Silence for Three Seconds*
> *Her:* "Well, it really hurt and I'm feeling mad!"
> *Me:* "OK, I'm sorry! What else can I say?" (A shift to Option 3: the conversation-ending apology)
> *Silence for Thirty Minutes*

During the second, longer silence, I became acutely aware that I had somewhere missed the road to Spirit Oneness. My wife and I were not experiencing a deep sense of our worth in Christ that enabled us to be mutually and sensitively responsive to each other's needs. I reflected on the fact that I really am a worthwhile person because of the Lord's love and purposes for me, whether or not I have been a success as a husband, and that my worth in Christ should be expressed not in retreat, but in an effort to minister to my wife. I approached her again, this time with a *different goal*. Before, I wanted to avoid pain by defending myself; now I determined to understand better what had happened and how I had hurt her in order to love her better in the future. Our second interchange went as follows:

> *Me:* "Honey, I really hurt you tonight. I guess I don't understand why what I said was so painful—but I want to. Will you talk to me about it?"
>
> *Her:* "I'm not sure I can. It still hurts a lot."
>
> *Me:* "I can accept that. I want to do a better job of making you feel loved. I failed you badly tonight, and I want to learn from it."
>
> *Her:* "I know you love me and are committed to making me feel good—but sometimes you seem so insensitive. I guess I really need to feel . . ."

And we talked for nearly an hour about our deepest needs and how we can be used of God to touch each other with healing rather than hurt. As we did so, we moved toward Spirit Oneness, the kind of profound closeness that results from meeting at the level of deepest needs.

3

Soul Oneness:
Manipulation or Ministry?

A pastor and his wife were approached by the elders of the church with a matter of deep concern. For nearly a year, undercurrents of dissatisfaction with the pastor's effectiveness had been rippling through the congregation. Clearly, something was wrong, but no one could pinpoint the difficulty. During recent months, however, a disturbing consensus was emerging among the church's leaders that the problems were somehow related to the pastor's marriage.

When the elders met to think through the situation, they agreed that the pastor's wife had been more and more consumed by her ministry of counseling troubled teen-agers. They wondered if perhaps this ministry so drained her energy that little was left for her ministry as a wife. It appeared that the more her counseling ministry grew, the more her husband had crowded his schedule with meetings, administrative duties, and routine responsibilities. The net effect seemed to be that he was losing the vital contact with people that he needed to serve the church effectively.

Although no one understood precisely how the pastor's retreat from his shepherding role related to his wife's preoccupation with counseling, the elders agreed that something in the marriage warranted attention. When they expressed their concerns to the couple at a special meeting, both reacted with chagrin and indignation. There were some tense moments, and firm exhortation was required before they would agree to seek counsel.

27

A few weeks later they entered my office, extending warm greetings to try to disguise their nervousness. I began by telling them that the elders had written me a letter stating their observations and concerns. The pastor vehemently stated his disagreement with the elders' conjectures and assured me that his marriage was as solid as ever and very much Christ-centered. His wife affirmed that she deeply loved her husband and had always put the home before her other ministries.

Our conversation revealed that this couple sincerely felt that they loved the Lord. They both evidenced strong knowledge of Christ's unconditional love as the basis of security and Christ's eternal purposes as the framework within which to find significance. Yet, though their hold on the truth went far beyond mere assent, I sensed that something important was missing. There was no spark of closeness between them, no spontaneity, no shared warmth, at best a stiff and well-protected friendliness.

In counseling, I usually encourage husband and wife to discuss specific recent events in their lives so that I can observe patterns of interaction. The pastor described a recent occasion when the couple enjoyed a rare evening out at a favorite restaurant. While they dined, his wife was called away to counsel a runaway girl who had just been picked up by the police. I asked the pastor how he felt as his wife left the table to deal with the emergency.

He smiled and answered, "She really has a heart for those kids. God has given her a unique and important ministry."

I continued, "I wonder if you ever wish that she would just relax with you during an evening without doing something related to her ministry and give you her full and undivided attention?"

"Oh, I suppose," he replied. "But I believe that what she does is truly important. And we've both dedicated our lives to whatever service God has for us."

At this point the wife fretted, "I don't agree with what I think you're getting at. My husband is more important to me than anything or anyone else except for God and His work. I happen to believe that God made us into a team who can minister to others. My husband pastors the church, and I offer what help I can to the kids God brings me. For the life of me, I can't see what is wrong with that."

Do this couple have a problem, or don't they? Does their marriage fit into God's design for oneness? They appear to understand that their needs are met in God, and they are dedicated to His service. Yet the relationship between them seems to be out of focus. What's wrong?

The Concept of Soul Oneness

Many evangelical couples can more or less articulate the essential thinking involved in Spirit Oneness: Christ is all I need for security and significance; therefore I don't need to depend on my spouse to meet my needs, and I can devote my life to sacrificial giving, believing that the Lord will replenish my resources when they run dry. Some couples understand that because of God's promises, they can jump from the Cliff of Safety into the Abyss of Rejection, counting only on the Rope of the Love of Christ to protect them when others let them down.

But for probably a majority of Christians, these truths are academic. Too often, couples have not actively thought through the radical implications of these concepts for the marital relationship. And because they do not translate them from theory into experience, these truths never become vital. The only truths that eventually grip a Christian at the core of his being are the turths by which he consistently lives.

The concepts behind Spirit Oneness lead naturally and necessarily into a style of husband-wife relating that I call "Soul Oneness."

When the Bible speaks of people exercising their capacity to relate to God, it often refers to them as *spirits* or it talks about the *spiritual* nature of mankind (e.g., see John 4:24). But ". . . when the word soul is used to refer to the non-material being of man, it generally designates the man in some relationship to earthly circumstances."[1]

In explaining Spirit Oneness, my primary focus is on each partner's individual relationship to God and on how that spiritual relationship reaches into a person's needs for security and significance. But when our attention shifts to husbands and wives relating to each other, the term *Soul Oneness* seems an appropriate conceptual label.

As I understand God's design, the Spirit Oneness that couples can enjoy is intended to lead to a further interpersonal (or soul) oneness. This oneness grows from a *mutual, intelligent, and unreserved commitment to be an instrument of God to deeply touch a spouse's personal needs in a unique, powerful, and meaningful way.* Or, more simply, if the foundation of Spirit Oneness is mutual dependence on the Lord for personal needs, then the foundation of Soul Oneness is a mutual commitment to minister to one another's personal needs.

Like so many Christian couples, the pastor and his wife had no clear understanding of a relationship of mutual ministry. In fact, careful analysis revealed that their marriage was built on a primary commitment, not to minister to each other, but rather to maneuver themselves into a relationship of minimum emotional pain. Neither partner had any substantial awareness of either (1) The profound needs hidden beneath the other's spiritually acceptable facade, or (2) Their incredible potential and opportunity for powerfully ministering to those deep needs.

There was a barrier between the couple that effectively blocked meaningful touching. The wall functioned much like

---

[1] J. Oliver Buswell, *A Systematic Theology of the Christian Religion* (Grand Rapids: Zondervan, 1972), part II, pp. 239-40.

a glass window between two people wanting to kiss: all of the proper motions were there, but none of the excitement—just cold glass. Only a deliberate shift from the subtle *commitment to manipulate* to the deliberate *commitment to minister* will shatter that barrier and permit the rich, intimate, fulfilling relationship of Soul Oneness. Let us see what this means.

What is Your Real Goal?

Everything we do has a goal. We are not conditioned animals that act automatically and unthinkingly in a programed response. Neither are we the hapless victims of internal, psychological forces that drive us relentlessly in unwanted directions. Although it may often *feel* as though we do things we don't want to do, the truth is that everything we do represents an effort to reach a goal that somehow, perhaps at an unconscious level, makes good sense to us.

Imbedded in our make-up are certain beliefs about how to become worthwhile or how to avoid injury to our self-esteem, how to be happy or how to avoid pain. As children, we acquire ideas about life from observing our parents (what makes them happy, why they feel bad), our teachers, television, and the like.

Because Satan is the prince of this world and because our fallen nature is naturally attracted to life plans that disregard God, each of us reliably develops *wrong beliefs* about how to find the meaning and love we need. And a belief about what I need implies a goal that I should pursue. If I *believe* I need food to live, I will make it my *goal* to get to the grocery store. *Beliefs determine goals*.

Suppose a boy is reared by parents who neglect him to pursue their own interests. He may develop the belief that there is no one who will attend to his needs. That wrong belief may lead him to strive for *absolute self-reliance* as the goal he must achieve to avoid personal pain.

31

Note how this concept of goals relates to marriage. Consider the following situations:

> *Situation 1:* After the children are in bed, a husband rests his hand on his wife's thigh and says, "Honey, you're really gorgeous, and I love you."
>
> *Situation 2:* As her husband leaves the dinner table and begins stuffing his briefcase full of business papers, the wife asks, "Do you have to go back to the office again tonight?"
>
> *Situation 3:* After a long day with three young children, mother impatiently snaps at the oldest for failing to do an assigned chore. Dad looks up from behind his newspaper and says, "Honey, jumping all over him isn't going to help!"

Suppose I were to ask each speaker in these vignettes to state the *goal* or purpose of his or her comment. The romantic husband in Situation 1 might say, "To let my wife know I love her." The disappointed wife in Situation 2 might offer, "I just want him to be more a part of our family." And the helpful husband in Situation 3 would likely suggest, "I want to give her some perspective on what she's doing. I regard it as part of my role as spiritual leader to help her do the best job she can as wife and mother."

As we attempt to specify the motivation that should characterize our interactions with our mates, we should remember that we will fail to see the point clearly and to make needed personal application without the Holy Spirit's help. The deceitfulness of our hearts renders us incapable of accurately identifying our real goals without supernatural help.

In its fallen state the human consciousness is a marvelous instrument of self-deception. It is capable of selectively attending to only those motives that preserve our cherished image of ourselves as good and kind and of disowning or at least disguising the ugly, self-centered objectives to which we are really committed. Only the Spirit of God unfolding His truth as revealed in Scripture can cut through our lying hearts to expose our selfish motivation. Therefore we must continually open ourselves to His enlightening work, or we will miss the entire purpose of this chapter: to uncover the hidden and destructive objectives that guide the interactions of so many couples.

Think about the three vignettes. In Situation 1, the amorous husband may be communicating a message obvious to his wife: "I want sex." If he were to be told this, he might defend his goal as sanctioned by Paul's instructions to married couples not to defraud one another sexually (1 Cor. 7:1-5). Perhaps he would appeal to his legitimate desire for a supportive, affectionate wife. When stripped to the core, however, his goal is to manipulate his wife to respond to him in a way that *he* desires, with little or at best secondary concern for *her* need to feel loved and appreciated rather than pressured and used.

One husband responded to this idea, "But my wife has no reason to feel rejected or unloved. I *do* love her! I just want her to be more affectionate. Is that so wrong?"

Clearly, there is nothing wrong and everything right with a warm, sensual, physical relationship. There is nothing wrong with desiring sex and hoping for a responsive wife— and making his desire known to his wife. But to be *primarily motivated* by the goal of winning a response from one's spouse that is designed to satisfy one's own desires, however legitimate those desires may be, is a violation of love and therefore wrong. Love is essentially defined in terms of preoccupation with the *other's* needs. The central goal of every interchange between partners must be to minister to the other's deepest needs for security and significance. I may legitimately *desire* a particular response from my wife. But if my spouse for whatever reason fails to respond as I wish, then I must honor my goal of ministry through an uncomplaining, nonpressuring acceptance of my disappointing spouse. This acceptance would be motivated by my awareness of her deep needs for love and by my commitment to do all that I can do to touch those needs.

When a husband replaces the goal of ministry on behalf of the other with the goal of manipulation on behalf of oneself, he is guilty of a serious misrepresentation of Christ's love for His bride.

Consider Situation 2. When the wife softly inquires, "Do you have to go back to work again tonight?" what do you think is her real goal? Her not-so-hidden purpose is to somehow persuade her husband to remain at home. As she pursues this objective, notice that her essential focus is not on her husband's need for respect and acceptance, but rather on her desire that he satisfy her longings.

"But," she retorts to the confronting counselor, "he is rarely at home with the kids. They miss him terribly and have told me so! Don't you agree that a father should spend time with his attention-starved kids? Isn't that a part of his Christian responsibility?"

The answer, of course, is Yes. But her comment misses the point. The issue for the wife to consider is not "What should my husband do?" but rather "What should be my primary goal as I interact with him?" Her central purpose when she asks her husband to stay home is far more than to express her longings; this woman's real goal is to manipulate her husband to do what she believes he should. My concern lies with her motivation and not the rightness of the response she wants from her husband. In her efforts to persuade him to do what she thinks best, there is no thought of sacrificial ministry to his need for a sense of adequacy and respect. Her motivation, therefore, is wrong and her actions will move the marriage further away from Soul Oneness.

The husband in Situation 3 who reprimands his wife for speaking harshly to their child seems aware only of his wife's *error* and is inattentive to her *needs*. His goal apparently was to correct her error, not to minister to her. If we had tape-recorded his brain as he listened to his wife scold their

34

youngster, it is unlikely that the tape would have picked up words like "I think my wife is handling our child incorrectly, but I want to be careful that I communicate neither rejection nor criticism to my wife. Above all else, I want her to know that I love her."

Because he did not have the conscious intention to minister, his real goal was to communicate his displeasure to his wife in the hope that she would speak more kindly to the child. Whenever the goal of our behavior is essentially to change the other person—whether the change is good or bad—we are wrong. Unless there is the purpose of communicating love based on an awareness of our spouses' needs, we qualify as manipulators, not ministers. *The key to achieving Soul Oneness is to maintain the fundamental goal of ministry to our partner's deepest needs and to keep that goal inviolate.*

The Principle of Ministry

Paul instructs us in Ephesians 4:29: "Do not let any unwholesome talk come out of your mouths, but only what is helpful or consistent with the goal of building others up according to their needs, that it may benefit those who listen."

The word translated "unwholesome" signifies something worthless that rots and decays. Paul is contrasting worthless words with words that last because they have a clear purpose: to meet the needs of others.

I believe Paul lays down here a core principle of relating that must govern interaction between all Christians. Certainly this principle applies to those who live together in the intimacy of marriage. I am to say nothing that in any way compromises the basic goal of ministering to the needs of the one to whom I am speaking. When I utter words with the *goal* of changing the other person without primary and conscious concern for his or her welfare, then those words are worthless. They serve no eternal purpose and will decay.

In marriage, words that do not comfortably fit within

35

a commitment to minister are foreign to God's design and will not yield the dividends of increasing Soul Oneness. The romantic husband may persuade his wife to have sex; the unhappy wife may convince her husband to stay home; the rebuking husband may pressure his wife into never raising her voice toward the children in his presence—but the gain will not be toward oneness. There will be a change, and the change may appear to be an improvement, but the longed-for sense of intimate closeness will not develop.

Let me now state more fully the principle of ministry on which Soul Oneness depends:

> Husbands and wives are to regard marriage as an opportunity to minister in a unique and special way to another human being, to be used of God to bring their spouses into a more satisfying appreciation of their worth as persons who are secure and significant in Jesus Christ.

Notice an essential point in this principle: It is Christ who provides us with security an significance. My love for my wife does not in the slightest degree add to the reality that she is thoroughly and eternally secure in Christ's love. Nor does my failure to love her as I should diminish the fact of her security. But my tangible, touchable, physically present love can bring to my wife a *deeper, experienced awareness of what it means to be loved.* I cannot add to the *fact* of her security, but I can add to her *feelings* of security.

Similarly, my wife's submissive respect for me does not increase my significance as a servant of Christ, but it does enrich my awareness of the adequacy that the Lord has already granted. The situation is much like a man who discovers that there is oil beneath my property. He does not make me wealthy; I was rich before he found the oil, but it is not until he makes me aware of the oil that I experience my wealth. Husbands do not make wives secure; wives do not make husbands significant. Only Christ can do this. And

He does so the moment a person places his or her trust in Him as Savior and Lord. But husbands and wives can help convince their partners of their value and bring them to fuller enjoyment of their riches in Christ.

The Principle of Manipulation (and How It Destroys Soul Oneness)

To understand better why the principle of ministry is the necessary foundation for developing rich marital oneness, consider an example of how its opposite (the principle of manipulation) can ruin a relationship.

Mary's parents were divorced when she was seven years old. After her father left home, he rarely visited Mary and showed little evidence of loving concern. Mary's mother never quite recovered from the divorce and, for most of Mary's growing-up years, was preoccupied with scraping together enough money to live and finding enough pleasure to make her life worth living. Understandably Mary never felt loved. She developed the belief that to find the happiness that eluded her mother, she needed to marry a strong, loving man who would involve himself deeply in her life. Beneath this need for love rumbled a quiet, nagging fear: "Will I ever find the love I need?" We may draw a circle to represent Mary as a personal being who at her core experiences profound fear. Let a minus sign denote her fearful insecurity.

Bob's dad was a highly successful lawyer who, in the way he spent his time, clearly evidenced that he valued prestige and position above all else. From Bob's youthful perspective, his dad's business position seemed to bring him a great deal of satisfaction. As Bob observed this, he formed the belief that a personally worthwhile existence depends on success. Through high school and college, Bob nursed a private fear that he might not be able to reach his goal of extraordinary financial and positional achievement. We may draw Bob's personal circle with a minus sign in the center to represent his fear that he might not be able to achieve his chosen goal.

Reflect on the psychological condition of these two people who would one day marry. Mary believed that security required relationship with a strong, faithful man quite unlike her father; her goal, therefore, became to find that man and to draw her security from him. Bob believed that significance would come from success, but he was unsure of his ability to attain the success he thought he needed; his goal, therefore, was first to regard himself as adequate and then to pursue business achievement.

During their courtship, Mary delighted in Bob's attention, listened intently to every word he said, laughed convincingly at every joke, and expressed admiration for his many good traits. He appeared to Mary to be a strong, self-assured, motivated, and loving man.

Bob felt good around Mary and concluded therefore that he had fallen in love. But what Bob mistakenly called love was in fact nothing more than an attraction to a woman who strengthened his sense of adequacy.

Mary wrongly interpreted Bob's warm interest as genuine love and regarded him as a means to realize the security she had desired for so long and feared would never come. Her feelings of intimacy with Bob were based entirely on what she thought Bob would do for her and not on expecting to make a positive impact on Bob's life.

Because each was looking to the other to provide for their personal needs, their tic-on-a-dog relationship could not develop Spirit Oneness. And because their motivations were self-centered, they missed the Principle of Ministry and were building their relationship on the Principle of Manipulation. Look at how manipulative motivation blocked the development of Soul Oneness.

Within the first few months of marriage, Mary, like all new brides, was hurt by her husband on several occasions. A specially prepared meal did not receive the expected praise;

his negative attitude toward helping around the house seemed to demean her work; her desire just to be warmly held ended often, at Bob's insistence, in the bedroom; a scratched auto fender earned a withering comment. Each experience of hurt struck deeply into her personal circle, and her dormant fear of rejection revived: "Will this relationship bring me pain? I could not endure the disappointment of having my hopes for love so quickly dashed."

To quiet the growing fear, Mary wrapped herself in protective layers designed to avoid more hurt. She became increasingly preoccupied with her own needs and lacked any motivation to minister to Bob's needs. She began thinking: "If I can just get him to be a little more loving, or if I can manage to keep our relationship distant enough so his rejection won't hurt as much, then perhaps I can minimize the pain." And so her goal became to control the relationship in a way designed to meet or to protect her needs. The principle of manipulation was fully in gear. She then began to drop comments like "Honey, I wish you'd just hug me without always making it into a sexual thing" or "You don't appreciate me at all" or "You don't treat me the way you did before we married." Beneath these "honest expressions of her feelings" (the misguided and destructive core of many unspiritual attempts to build a relationship) lay the hidden but forceful purpose to avoid further hurt. Their marriage now looked like this:

Shift the focus to Bob. His purpose in marrying Mary was also manipulative: he wanted to feel better about himself in order to promote the confidence he needed to succeed. When Mary started to communicate that he was not measuring up to her expectations, his feelings of adequacy weakened and his fear of never reaching his goal of success intensified. When people hurt, their immediate goal is to lessen the pain. So Bob began protecting himself from facing his feared inadequacy by retreating from Mary. His goal became to remove himself from the prospect of further hurt.

Never once would his urgent attention to his own needs permit any real concern for Mary's needs; his fear consumed him. He too was operating according to the principle of manipulation.

The vicious cycle has begun: The more Bob retreats, the more Mary's fear of rejection increases. The more her fear increases, the more she attempts to manipulate Bob to protect herself. The more she tries to change him, the more she communicates that Bob is failing and the more his sense of inadequacy grows. The more inadequate he feels around Mary, the more he retreats. The more he retreats, the more her fear increases. The dreary cycle continues until two lonely people find themselves hopelessly trapped behind thick walls of their own making that keep them from ever really touching each other. The tragedy is that these people are not merely two misguided souls longing for intimacy; they are also self-centered people so committed to the principle of manipulation that their walls will likely remain in place until they divorce or die. Neither partner entertains the faintest thought of being used of God to meaningfully reduce the other's fear.

There is only one escape from this self-made prison, and that is to completely rebuild the relationship on a radically different premise. Both partners must change their goals from manipulation to ministry. And the revolution requires supernatural intervention. Otherwise it cannot succeed.[2]

Changing Goals

The power of God is indispensable to altering one's commitments meaningfully. Until I am aware that my needs are already met in Christ, I will be motivated by emptiness

---

[2]Marriage counseling that does not concern itself fundamentally with changing the goals of husband and wife from manipulation to ministry and that fails to bring spiritual resources to bear in accomplishing this task amounts to nothing more than instruction in congenial manipulation.

to meet my needs. When by simple faith I accept Christ's shed blood as full payment for my sins, I am brought into a relationship with an infinite Being of love and purpose who fully satisfies my deepest needs for security and significance. Therefore I am freed from self-centered preoccupation with my own needs; they are met. It is now possible for me to give to others out of my fullness rather than needing to receive from others because of my emptiness. For the first time, I have the option of living selflessly.

Consider how this supernatural change in our goals can occur once the foundation of justification is in place. From a human perspective, three elements are required to shift from manipulation to ministry:

> *Element 1.* A decisive and continuous willingness to adopt the commitment to minister;
>
> *Element 2.* A substantial awareness of your partner's needs;
>
> *Element 3.* A conviction that you are God's chosen instrument to touch those needs.

Element 1: A decision to minister

The commitment to minister does not evolve naturally. To develop the right motivation, more is required than time spent in the Bible, sincere prayer, and the study of good Christian literature. Although a consistent devotional life is necessary for the shift to be lasting and thorough, the path from manipulation to ministry centrally involves a deliberate choice, or better, a series of deliberate choices. Selfless motivation is not developed by passively "letting go and letting God." The Spirit of God quickens our mind and our wills, enabling us to repent and obey. First, I must agree with God that manipulation to meet my own needs is sinful. I must turn from my sin, believing that a good God leads me along good paths (repent). Then I must choose to walk along the path of ministry (obey).

41

All of us face various character-molding decisions every day. To speak with my spouse, I must consciously and deliberately *think*: "My purpose right now must be to help my wife realize her value as a person. What can I do that will accomplish this?" My insides may urgently scream with a compelling desire to defend myself, criticize her, or make other manipulative responses. Amid this inner turmoil, I must make a decision to do what will help her feel loved. As I make the choice, the Spirit of God provides the power to make it real—but I must make the choice.

The natural resistance to truly giving ourselves to the other is rooted in our stubborn fear that if we really give, with no manipulative purpose, we will be shortchanged. Our needs will not be met. At best we'll be disappointed; at worst, we'll be destroyed.

But God is faithful. We are to trust His perfect love to cast out our fear, believing that as we give to our spouses in His name, He will supernaturally bless us with an awareness of His presence. And He will. But it may take time—perhaps months—before we sense His work in us. The willingness to give unconditionally does not come by simply deciding to be selfless. The stain of self-centeredness requires many washings before it no longer controls our motivation. Many commitments to minister and much time spent with God will transpire before we know what it means to *give*. Our job is to learn faithfulness and to press on in obedience, not giving in to discouragement or weariness, believing that God will always honor the conscious and persevering motivation to serve Him. When a spouse becomes more critical, drinks more heavily, or rejects efforts of ministry, we are to continue in our obedience, believing that our responsibility before God is to obey and to trust Him for the outcome.

Element 2: An awareness of your partner's needs

Think again of the pastor and his wife whose marriage was friendly but neither intimate nor rewarding. Much of my counseling involved encouraging each partner to become aware of his or her own aching needs and then expose those needs to the other.

I am convinced that most husbands and wives have little awareness of the intense yearnings crying from their partners' hearts. Too often, one of the protective layers people hide behind is the layer of "apparent togetherness" of "I can handle things" or "I'm O.K. and I assume you're O.K." Confident smiles coupled with spiritual platitudes about "all things working for good" often mask a deep longing to be accepted. We fervently desire someone to know us as we are—worried, shattered, scared, angry, lustful—and to accept us anyway.[3]

Therefore I regard an honest sharing of who I am with my spouse as consistent with the principle of ministry. I am not to complain about how bad I feel; rather, I am to remind myself that my needs are met in Christ and to share with my spouse how I feel in our relationship. My goal in sharing is to vulnerably reveal myself, legitimately desiring, but never demanding, a loving response.

Element 3: A conviction that you are God's chosen minister to your spouse

So many of us struggle with a sense of inadequacy and incompetence that it is difficult to believe that we have the resources to bear fruit in our ministry of marriage. Relationships are complicated. People are complicated. We may feel stupid, unable to figure out exactly what we should do: "No matter what I do, it makes no difference to her." "He is such a puzzle to me. I just don't know what to do when he gets like that. Everything I try flops."

Books have been written on principles of effective ver-

---

[3]In our culture some folks make a fetish of displaying their miserable insides. Clearly, there are two extremes to be avoided: fearful hiding and indiscriminate exhibitionism.

bal interaction. I have read several. Yet I still find myself stumped sometimes when I face relationship problems that the principles do not seem to cover. Christians are called upon to believe that in spite of our confusion and incompetence, our sovereign God has made no mistake in assigning us the ministry of touching our spouses' deepest needs. Regardless of the circumstances under which people were married, God affords each married partner a unique opportunity to minister in a special way to his or her mate.

Now, with all three elements for change solidly in place, it is possible to begin to shift from manipulation to ministry. Consider an example of how it's done. Remember that unless we deliberately adopt the goal of ministry on a moment-by-moment basis, our natural, reflexive goal will generally be to manipulate our spouses for our advantage.

Fred enters his home after a long day at work. His automatic, unplanned, and perhaps unconscious goal likely involves a desirable response from his wife Joan, perhaps a friendly greeting, a warm hug, or a prepared dinner. Suppose she welcomes him by asking, "Why are you so late? You said you'd be home by six and it's nearly seven."

Joan has blocked Fred's goal. Reflect for a moment. How do people *feel* when their goal is blocked? Most often, they become angry or at least frustrated. Fred feels anger toward his wife. He admits to himself that he feels like retorting with a snappy comment like "Hey, thanks for the warm welcome! Sure is nice to come home!"

What should he do? His options are (1) to express his anger, (2) to defend his late arrival, (3) simply to ignore Joan's comment and wash up for dinner, or (4) to soothe her with a warm embrace. Remember the essential point of the chapter. Soul Oneness depends on our *motives* for what we do more than on the specifics of *what we do*. The question Fred needs to ask is not *"What should I do?"* but rather *"What is my goal?"*

Fred's anger should be a strong warning that his goal

was manipulative. He was demanding a response from his wife that would meet his need of the moment. If Fred is (1) committed to the principle of ministry, (2) aware of his wife as a woman who longs to feel loved, and (3) convinced that he is God's instrument to tangibly represent Christ's love to his wife, then he is able to change his goal. The actual operation involves replacing thoughts like "Why can't she be pleasant when I come home?" to "My goal right now is to let my wife know that she is a loved and special woman."

Think again of the mind as a tape recorder. The automatic "tape" we play reflects our manipulative goal of changing our spouse: "Why can't she greet me warmly?" To change goals, we must decisively eject that wrong tape and insert a new one into position, that is, choose a new sentence to reflect our changed goal: "I want to make her feel loved."

Changing tapes must be more than a mechanical procedure. As we replace our selfish thoughts with giving intentions, we need to remind ourselves that we are freely choosing to minister because we believe God. Although our feelings may not immediately shift from anger to compassion, we can convey noncritical acceptance to our spouses if ministry is our freely selected purpose.

The crux of the matter is, Do we really want to accept the goal of ministry at this moment? The more we are willing to do so, the more surely our marriage will move toward satisfying levels of Soul Oneness.

4

Body Oneness: Physical Pleasure with Personal Meaning

If poor communication heads the list of marital complaints, sexual problems run a close second. Nowhere does disharmony between spouses express itself more painfully than in the bedroom.

Here is a sampling of the concerns I hear regularly in my counseling:

> "I feel so used by my husband. When he wants sex, he expects me to be ready at a moment's notice. And he never will stop at just hugging me. We always end up in the bedroom. It's made me pull away from him physically."

> "I can't understand why my wife is so unresponsive. I'd settle for a warm kiss once in a while, but at best all I get is mechanical cooperation. It sure makes it hard not to look somewhere else for satisfaction. I can't understand why she isn't more willing to meet my sexual needs."

> "I've never had an orgasm, I don't think. And I feel terrible about it! I guess I feel cheated when I see how much my husband enjoys his climax. And to make it worse, I can't tell him the truth—I fake an orgasm. He'd be really upset if he knew he doesn't satisfy me."

Imagine yourself in the role of the counselor. What would you do to help these people? What are the problems behind their sexual difficulties: poor technique, insecurity, psychological hang-ups, selfishness, different levels of sex drive? Exactly what *should* a Christian couple experience in the privacy of their bedroom?

So far in this book, I have suggested that an intimate relationship between husband and wife is nourished by the growth of *Spirit Oneness*, a turning to the Lord rather than to one's spouse to find security and significance, and *Soul Oneness*, a commitment to minister to the spouse's needs rather than manipulating to meet one's own needs.

The goal of oneness in marriage involves a third element. This element is too often regarded as central to a relationship, but it is happily necessary to complete the biblical picture of marital oneness. A human being is not only a *Spirit* capable of relating personally to God, and a *Soul* able to relate personally to other people, but also a *Body*, a physical being equipped with five senses for relating as a body to other bodies. We can *touch* each other's bodies, *smell* them, often *see* and *hear* the noises they make, and even *taste* them. People can interact with their bodies.

Just as God has graciously provided instructions for our personal relationships, so has He also communicated a special design for our physical relationships. Following this design will result in a pleasurable and meaningful sexual relationship between husband and wife. In this chapter I will first explain what Body Oneness is and then tell how it can be developed.

Body Oneness vs. Fun Sex

As I read the romantic story in the Song of Solomon and meditate on the intended richness of the marriage union—so rich that it serves as a living parable of the bond between Christ and His bride—I cannot help but think that Christian couples are short-changing themselves when all they want from their sexual relationship is more pleasure and less frustration. I am not suggesting that we pursue some sort of "spiritualized sex" untouched by sheer sensual plea-

47

sure, but I do believe our sexual make-up equips us to enjoy much more than a really good climax. To splash about in a puddle when God provides an ocean is no noble self-denial. It is worse than foolish. It not only robs us of intended blessing, but robs God of glory and the joy of giving.

Let me clarify this by making a distinction between Body Oneness and what I call "Fun Sex." As is his custom, Satan has counterfeited what God offers to committed Christians. It is quite clear—and the testimony of thousands affirms—that the only requirement for sexual pleasure is the proper positioning of two cooperative bodies. No emotional relationship between the two persons is needed. A man once told me that while he was in the service, he had sexual relations with dozens of women and never knew even one of them by name. Yet the sex itself was physically pleasurable to him. When I refer to sheer physical pleasure as Fun Sex, I am simply contrasting it with Frustrating, Dull, Tension-filled Sex. In no way do I suggest that only sinful sex can be fun.

Body Oneness is different from Fun Sex—and better. I use the term to refer to a physical relationship that a Christian couple can enjoy who know something of the reality of Spirit and Soul Oneness. The distinction can be stated simply: Fun Sex involves physical pleasure without legitimate personal meaning. Body Oneness involves physical pleasure with personal meaning. Let me develop these concepts.

Fun Sex

Something has gone wrong with the sexual drive. The natural appetite for erotic pleasure has become a mad tyrant, demanding fulfillment with no concern for either boundaries or consequences. Ruined reputations, shattered relationships, prematurely ended ministries—no price seems too high to pay for the pleasures of sex. Why? Why has the biological desire for sexual fun become a slavemaster, driving people to disregard God's standards?

One of the great errors of our day is the growing tendency to think of people as nothing more then intricate and self-conscious organizations of physical matter, collections of chemicals that come together during gestation and disintegrate after death. Words like *soul* and *spirit* are largely devoid of any substantive meaning and serve only as inspiring rhetoric to elegantly describe how the human machine functions. Nothing exists but matter—bones, organs, skin, and hair.

Something called the "human potential movement" has rightly rebelled against such dehumanizing theory, insisting that people are more than mortal bodies. We are persons, say the humanists, real persons whose worth and value cannot be reduced to our material nature.

For many of us, the affirmation that we are more than machines has a certain appeal. A large segment of our society may be willing to regard a fetus as merely a bit of tissue, but somehow we rebel at the suggestion that the cooing infant in our arms is simply an emotional, squirming machine. Clearly, we want to think of people—at least the ones we like or value—as persons and not machines.

But there is a problem. If we refuse—as most humanists do—to believe that life began with a personal Creator, then all talk of people as more than impersonal, complex machines amounts to nothing more than satisfying delusion. For something impersonal to give birth to something personal is as reasonable as expecting a rock to evolve into a dog. To speak of the value of persons without a living, personal God as the ultimate beginning is folly.

With God out of the picture, there is neither basis for regarding ourselves as truly personal (more than bodies) nor resources to satisfy personal needs. If we are nothing more than physical machines, then we really have no personal needs.

The real tragedy of denying our character as persons made in the image of a personal God is that very few people are aware of the exhilarating potential for *personal* satisfaction. We have missed the truth that the deepest joys and satisfactions do not come through the five senses. Even Christians who really should know better try to relieve *personal* pain with *physical* pleasure. When we hurt from rejection, emptiness, fear, or loneliness, the temptation to gain relief by pleasantly arousing our physical senses is almost irresistible. We snack on potato chips when we're bored, climb into a hot tub when we're tense, masturbate when we feel alone—something, anything to replace the ache in our hearts with good feelings.

No bodily sensation is quite so intensely pleasurable or all-consuming as sexual arousal and release. If we regard ourselves merely as bodies and if we therefore want more than anything else to find some way to feel physically good, then sex is the ticket. And the pursuit of sexual pleasure can become a strong preoccupation. The compulsive craving for erotic excitement prevalent in our society is rooted in our denial of ourselves as real persons made for personal fellowship with God and others.

But—rather than relieving or resolving the personal problems that result from rejection or criticism, sexual pleasure merely camouflages the pain with physical sensations. The situation is like a man with a brain tumor getting drunk: although he feels no pain, he is still dying.

The unresolved personal disorder—a lack of security and significance—still clamors for attention. And the demand is often felt as a strong urge to experience even more physical pleasure. A vicious circle is set into motion: the anesthesia of sexual pleasure for personal pain drives the pain out of awareness where it is experienced no longer as a *personal* problem but as an urge for more *physical* pleasure; more pleasure then renders the pain less recognizable as personal and increases its felt demand for physical relief, which leads to further sexual experiences—and on to the point of absolute degeneracy. What begins as an effort to relieve a problem ends not in real solutions but additional problems. Guilt, rationalization, further enslavement to inner urges, unanswered personal questions—the wages of sin is death. The way seems right, but the end is personal destruction.

My major point is this: Sex provides a *physical* solution for a *personal* problem. The evil thing is that it seems to work so well. During those few magic moments of sexual climax, a person experiences a consuming excitement in the body that counterfeits a sense of wholeness in the soul. Satan's most convincing imitation of the enduring and real *personal* worth available in Christ is the temporary but intense *bodily* pleasure of sex. He seeks to persuade us that when our bodies are tingling with sexual excitement, we have reached the ultimate in our potential for satisfaction—there is nothing deeper to be enjoyed. And his argument is convincing to the degree that we regard ourselves as mere bodies evolved from impersonal matter and not as real persons made in the image of a personal God.

So Satan does offer Fun Sex: sex that for a moment helps a woman feel desirable, feminine, wanted, secure; sex that enables a man to feel attractive, adequate, manly, significant. But Satan cannot offer meaningful relationship built on loving commitment to one another. Fun Sex is a charade. It satisfies the body but leaves the real person empty and despairing. It offers pleasure for the body without meaning for the person.

Body Oneness

God offers something more than Fun Sex. His design for Body Oneness provides us not only with the legitimate physical pleasure of sexual intimacy, but also with meaning. Body Oneness includes pleasure for the body *and* rich meaning for the person. Consider how this works.

Personal meaning in God's world depends finally on participation in God's purposes. To build something that has no eternal impact but will disappear like castles in the sand is *not* meaningful. But to have a part in erecting a structure

51

that will never crumble *is* meaningful. The marriage relationship is one of God's creations for building up people. It gives husbands and wives the chance to minister to an immortal human being in a uniquely intimate fashion. To enjoy the meaningfulness of marriage, then, requires a once-made but ongoing commitment of mutual ministry to build up our mates. The more we see opportunities to minister to our mates and the more we seize them, the more meaning our marriage will have. This is the Soul Oneness we examined earlier.

But while I am trying to minister to my wife's personal needs, I sense needs within me. It is at this point I must take very seriously the conviction that nearness to God is my only good, that He alone is sufficient to satisfy what I need to live as I should. Upon reckoning what is true—that I am secure and significant in Christ—I must by faith approach my wife as a personally full husband, willing to share the love shed abroad in my heart, needing nothing in return. When she reacts with loving respect, I feel great. When she reacts with something else like neglect or criticism or indifference, I will hurt—but I must hold firmly onto the truth that I am whole in Christ and therefore not threatened by my wife's response. The more that spouses react to each other on the basis of their perceived fullness in Christ, the more their marriage will progress toward Spirit Oneness.

A personally meaningful marriage depends on the development of Soul Oneness. And Soul Oneness cannot grow without Spirit Oneness. When both levels of oneness are present, the relationship is vital and intimate. Core parts of the personality are touched and engaged. Communication reaches beneath the routineness of "What's for supper?" or "Where shall we go on vacation?" or "Do you want to have sex? It's been a month." An awareness of unusual closeness develops, not in a steady rhythm, but in erratic outbursts that gradually diminish in intensity and increase in frequency toward a pattern of generally increasing unity. Then a couple, in their sexual activity, enjoy each other's body in the rich *personal* union that already exists. The phrase "make love" fits poorly. "Expressing love" is better. The Song of Songs celebrates the intoxicating pleasure of sexual activity between two persons who are united by loving commitment. The two *bodies* that come together house two *persons* who are already together.

I have defined Body Oneness as pleasure for the body and meaning for the person. Let me now offer a more complete description. Body Oneness is—

- Sexual pleasure between a couple who depend on the Lord to meet their needs and are committed to being used of God in meeting each other's needs;
- Sexual pleasure that grows out of a commitment to minister to one's spouse in the physical realm by giving maximum sexual pleasure;
- Sexual pleasure that provides a shared experience of sensual excitement and sexual satisfaction;
- Sexual pleasure that heightens each partner's awareness of their unbreakable bond.

Overcoming Obstacles to Body Oneness

If God intends that husbands and wives enjoy sex, why is it so often a source of argument, boredom, and disappointment rather than harmony, excitement, and fulfillment? If the philanderers of this world are to be believed, the Fun Sex available in the motel is far more enjoyable than the feeble attempts at Body Oneness in the marital bedroom. One husband told me that he was impotent with his Christian wife and erotically alive with his pagan girlfriend. To him, biblical morality was an invitation to a celibate life.

If the choice is between Fun Sex or Body Oneness, most people—Christian or not—would likely opt for sexual pleasure *with* personal meaning. But for many, the alternatives seem to be Fun Sex (pleasure without meaning) or

No Oneness (neither pleasure nor meaning). Small wonder that professing Christians in increasing numbers are stepping across the line of morality, leaving behind a bad relationship and sexual frustration in search of at least something that feels good.

Our society needs no reminder that sexual pleasure is available. People do not need a biblical relationship of marital oneness (or any sort of personal relationship) to enjoy Fun Sex. It is also clear—and discouraging to many Christian couples—that efforts to develop a personal relationship often seem to interfere with rather than to enhance sexual pleasure. When a couple engage in the hard work of opening up to each other while striving to work out their commitment to ministry, they open the door to conflicts, unhealed wounds, and unresolved tensions that sometimes act like water on sexual sparks.

Why should this be? God's design prohibits sex except in marriage. But the very effort to carry out the marriage vows by developing a close relationship gets in the way of sexual pleasure. Yet God wants us to experience the joys of sex within a growing personal relationship. The rest of this chapter explains why marriage can be the worst environment for experiencing sexual pleasure, but how we can make it the perfect environment for achieving Body Oneness.

In recent years, beginning with Masters and Johnson's controversial but enlightening research, much attention has been focused on human sexual responsiveness.[1] Emerging from this extensive research is the understanding that three overlapping kinds of problems have the potential to decrease sexual interest and interfere with the normal sexual pattern of arousal and orgasmic release. These problems are—

1. *Problems in the Person:* Personal hang-ups or psychological inhibitions often traceable to past experiences of

---

[1]William H. Masters and Virginia E. Johnson, *Human Sexual Responses* (Boston: Little, Brown & Co., 1966).

emotional pain that somehow involved sexuality (e.g., rape, incest, punishment for sexual curiosity);

2. *Problems Between the Partners:* Relational tensions stemming from communication problems, irritation and resentment, fear of rejection, guilt for past indiscretions, etc.;

3. *Problems With Technique:* Inadequate knowledge of how to relate sexually to a partner in a way that promotes desire, arousal, and climax.

Of all these, the problems with technique are most readily corrected. The other two kinds of problems involve more stubborn personal difficulties and require greater insight and painful emotional work to overcome. This is undoubtedly one reason why some people elect to travel the wide, smooth, short path to Fun Sex rather than the narrow, bumpy, longer road to Body Oneness.

Christians, of course, are not allowed this option. We are commanded to do the hard work of building a relationship as a foundation for our enjoyment of sex. Fun Sex is less than God intends for us; He never endorses a counterfeit. And He supplies the resources for us to walk the narrow road that leads to Body Oneness. But what are these resources? Let's look at the means Christ provides for overcoming these three obstacles to Body Oneness.

Problems in the Person

To my mind, all the problems that we label "emotional hang-ups" or "psychological disorders" are the symptoms of unmet personal needs. People who are afraid to trust anyone, to be open, to make decisions, or to relax rather than work have never understood deeply enough the security and significance available in Jesus Christ. Beneath the *appearance* of psychological problems is the *reality* of unmet needs for personal worth. These needs remain unmet because people find it difficult to take God at His word and act on the fact that in Christ they are both secure and significant. Consider an example.

A little girl is molested by her father. This confusing, painful experience may teach her that men are a source of hurt and must never be trusted. Perhaps she grows up believing that her security needs cannot be met and that it would be wise to protect herself from rejection by keeping some sort of distance between herself and men.

One day she marries. Her husband is looking forward to their first night together. When he approaches her, something happens: she freezes inside, she feels nervous, tight. Her husband struggles to be patient but cannot conceal his disappointment and frustration. She feels terrible. She wonders what is wrong with her. Time doesn't help. As the months pass, she withdraws from sexual involvement more and more, eager to avoid the emotional pain. Her husband tries a few lackluster seductions, then quits, and settles into a pattern of mechanical release whenever her guilt prompts her to "service" him. When this couple sit together in church, there is no warmth between them; a jointly held hymnbook is the extent of their oneness. Fulfilling, pleasurable sex seems like the impossible dream. The beginning of the tragedy is a Problem in the Person, in this case, the wife.

Notice the core of her problem. She is controlled by *fear* based on the *wrong belief* that if she gives herself to her husband, and if he in any way mistreats her, she would then be face to face with the pain of insecurity. Her problem must not be defined as the childhood molesting. Certainly that was terrible, but the real damage lay in its effect on what she *believes*. For years her life has been governed by the assumption that sexual closeness with a man contains a legitimate threat to her security as a woman.

But the assumption is simply not true. For the Christian, the basic need to be loved and to feel secure in a relationship is fully met in Christ. Yet this woman has not acted on the basis of that truth. She is still depending on her husband to provide her with security, but because of her belief that closeness means more insecurity, she has backed away from him, making Body Oneness impossible.

The solution here is *not* to gain greater confidence that her husband will not hurt her, but to challenge her belief that sexual closeness poses a valid threat to her need for love. If her need for love is truly met by the God of love, then rejection from her husband may be legitimately *painful* but not *threatening*. Her need for security remains fully met because of Christ's unchanging faithfulness.

On the strength of this correct belief, she must jump from her Cliff of Safety—to use the metaphor of chapter 2— into the Chasm of Whatever She Fears the Most, trusting only in the Lord's love to preserve her. In counseling, I would then ask her to *decide* that she will not avoid anything because of a fear of rejection. The next step would be to set up a program of deliberately choosing to do what she fears— the practical side of cliff-jumping. Perhaps she will need to reestablish some sort of relationship with her dad. Certainly she must approach her husband for sex: a homework assignment might be to snuggle up to him on the couch during a TV show rather than busying herself in the kitchen.

Thus, Problems in the Person can be thought of as evidence of unmet personal needs, which remain unmet because of (1) a refusal to believe that in Christ we are already secure and significant, and (2) a fear-motivated unwillingness to act on this belief by doing whatever scares us the most.

Problems Between the Partners

A second category of obstacles to Body Oneness involves problems of relationship between the persons. Even though the tensions between partners have their beginning in the individuals themselves, a whole set of problems needs to be remedied by them together.

When people do not depend fully on the Lord to satisfy their essential needs, they necessarily turn to others. Their purpose becomes to arrange their worlds of people and things in a way that brings some sense of satisfaction. The goal of manipulation—attempting to change whatever does not satisfy so that it will satisfy—is set in motion. Husbands try to make their wives lose weight, stop nagging, be more cooperative sexually, and acquiesce to their opinions. Wives work hard to get their husbands to play less golf, help more with housework, be more romantic, spend more time with the children, and share feelings more openly.

One key difficulty with these manipulative goals (which seem so reasonable—"After all, shouldn't he spend more time at home?") is that they all violate a cardinal rule of mental heath: *Never assume responsibility for a goal you cannot control*. No person can ever fully control the response of another. Influence yes, control no.

Suppose your spouse refuses to be manipulated. You cannot guarantee that your efforts to change the other will be effective. Perhaps, as often happens, pressure to change results in change—but change in a direction opposite to what is desired. What then?

When a goal is not reached, people experience either anxiety, resentment, or guilt. If a husband's goal is to gain his wife's respect for a certain decision he has made, and if she responds with bewildered disagreement ("You did *what*?"), he will likely feel angry and *resentful*. His wife has blocked his goal.

Suppose a wife's goal is to be treated gently and kindly. In the past, her husband has been known to make cutting comments about her in front of others. In a group, she is nervous about what he might say. Because her manipulative goal is precarious, she will feel *anxious*.

Consider a man raised by perfectionistic parents. He may set the goal of never disappointing his wife and children, believing that only by setting a consistent example of spiritual maturity can he regard himself as worthwhile. Whenever he thinks he has let his family down ("I know you're tired, dad, so we can play ball tomorrow"), this burdened man will feel *guilt*. Although his goal is unreachable, he will likely berate himself for failing to reach it.

These three toublesome emotions all tend to inhibit sexual arousal. It is difficult to feel angry with your spouse and sensual at the same time. If you are nervous around your partner, you will have trouble getting into the relaxed frame of mind vital to sexual interest. Similarly, a weight of guilt will block sexual excitement.

It is fair to say that problems between partners that inhibit enjoyable sex can be traced to manipulative goals. Communication difficulties, lack of time together, and failure to share openly can all be understood as the result of self-centered goals. The accompanying resentment, anxiety, and guilt that block the growth of Body Oneness are a part of this evil package of mutual manipulation.

If obviously will do no good to instruct an angry husband, a worried wife, or a guilt-ridden partner to feel different. The remedy is to change goals. Shift from manipulating your spouse to meet your needs to ministering to your spouse's needs. When this shift takes place, these debilitating emotions slowly give way to compassion and warmth. Why?

1. The goal of ministering cannot be blocked by your spouse. There is therefore no trigger for *resentment* toward your partner;

2. Fulfilling the goal of ministry depends only on your willingness. The *anxiety* of wondering what your mate will do is eliminated.

3. The goal of representing the Lord to your spouse is reachable, at least as a basic direction. Although everyone occasionally fails, the resources of confession, forgiveness, repentance, and enabling are available to get back on the track and grow in consistency. There is no warrant for self-preoccupying *guilt*.

Problems With Technique

Some couples are trusting God to meet their personal needs and are committed to mutual ministry, but still do not have a good sexual relationship. Sometimes the problem involves an insufficient or incorrect knowledge of the art of lovemaking.

In certain circles, one almost gets the impression that to know of the intricacies of sexual functioning and to be a romantic, skilled sexual partner is somehow less than spiritual. But ignorance of how to sexually arouse and satisfy one's spouse brings no glory to the One who created sex in the first place.

It is surprising how many men simply do not know what arouses and satisfies a woman. They lack awareness that the clitoris and not the vagina is her primary organ of sexual sensitivity, lack understanding of her need for warm and tender caresses, and lack appreciation for her desire for a romantic prelude rather than the "let's-go-do-it" approach.

On the other hand, many women fail to recognize the impact of visual stimuli such as provocative clothing. They do not understand the threat implied in their bored consent, mechanical servicing, or irritated turndowns. They may be ignorant of technical matters such as how to help a man delay his ejaculation.

Body Oneness, the experience of sexual pleasure that expresses the personal oneness of spirit and soul, is part of God's plan for total marital oneness. A marriage that is developing all three aspects of oneness—Spirit, Soul, and Body—provides a couple with a living parable of the eternal union of Christ and His bride, the church.

The goal of marriage, then, is—

● Spirit Oneness: Trusting in Christ alone to meet your personal needs for security and significance;

● Soul Oneness: Ministering to your partner in a way that enhances an awareness of his or her worth in Christ;

● Body Oneness: Enjoying sexual pleasure as an expression and outgrowth of a personal relationship.